"Seldom do I read business books written with the heart and soul of The Good Bus. Corliss McGinty (aka "HR Momma") gets it right, answering our most pressing questions on recruiting, hiring, and retention. Hop on board and get ready for the ride!"

—**Marshall Goldsmith**, million-selling author of the *New York Times* bestsellers *MOJO* and *What Got You Here Won't Get You There*

The Good Bus

THE GOOD BUS

Getting the Right People on Board Is Just the Beginning

By Corliss McGinty

Greensboro, North Carolina

Copyright © 2013 Corliss McGinty

All rights reserved. No portion of this book may be reproduced mechanically, electronically, or by any other means, including photocopying, without written permission of the publisher.

Interior Design by Imagine! Studios, LLC
www.ArtsImagine.com

Published by Soft Solutions Consulting, Inc.
Greensboro, North Carolina

ISBN 13: 978-0-9849645-1-2

First Soft Solutions Consulting, Inc. printing: March 2013

"Those who build great companies understand that the ultimate throttle on growth for any great company is not markets, or technology, or competition, or products. It is the one thing above all others; the ability to get and keep enough of the right people."

–Jim Collins, *Good to Great*

Table of Contents

Introduction xi

CHAPTER ONE: Getting the Right People on the Bus 1

   A Strong Employment Brand 3
      Application: The Unfortunate Reality 3
      Application: The Ideal 4
      And Another Thing…The Recruiting Process 5
   Choosing the Right Person for the Bus: The Hiring Process 5
      Have a Consistent Process 6
      Sourcing. 6
   Take Action 10

CHAPTER TWO: Getting the Right Person in the Right Seat . . 11

   Use Their Strengths to Keep Employees Engaged . . . 12
   Create a Job Profile 12
   The Interview Process 14
   Extending Offers 17
   Arriving at the Bus 18
   The Plan: Moving Forward 19
   And Now… A Little Advice for Employees 20
   Take Action 24

CHAPTER THREE: Getting Everyone Going to the Same Destination 25

   Healthy Doubts 27

Compensation 28
Time Off 30
    Netflix: Freedom and Responsibility Reign 31
    Best Buy: Results-Only Working Environment 32
Coaches, Mentors, and Development 34
    Feedback and Coaching 35
    Mentoring: It's Not What You Think It Is 36
Performance Reviews 40
Putting Conflict to Work 41
    Encouraging Your People to Speak up 43
Innovation & Creative Thinking 47
    Research about Creativity 47
    Time for Independent Thinking 48
"Grit" 51
Engagement 52
Purpose & Community 52
Take Action 54

CHAPTER FOUR: Singing Kumbaya (Keeping Those Happy Campers on the Bus) 55

Fun! 56
Community Involvement 58
Positivity 58
A Good Relationship with YOU: The Leader 60
Take Action 66

In Conclusion **67**

Appendix: Suggested Reading List **69**

Introduction

For 30 years, people have told me, "You have a way with words—you should write a book." Don't you love those "shoulds" people have for *your* life? In this case, though, I knew they were right. I enjoy writing, from journaling and *real* snail mail (handwritten on cool stationery) to blogs and columns in any publication that will allow me to speak my mind. Writing a book wasn't that far of a reach!

Like many other people, I fell into the HR arena several decades ago. There are so many of us who haven't really planned our careers. We've just been offered certain opportunities on our life path and decided to go for them! Surely my early training in fine art and psychology was in no way related to what I do now, is it? Of course it is! As a dabbler, I enjoy learning new things and having an occupation that allows me to enjoy varied activities and have fingers in many pies.

At Silicon Design Labs, the pioneering high-tech start-up I was working for in 1985, I had to choose between the *numbers* (I was doing financial statements like P&Ls, balance sheets,

A/P, A/R, payroll [ugh!], depreciation, and cost accounting) or the *people* (human resource responsibilities such as benefits, recruiting, employee parties, etc.), because in a few short years the company grew from 29 to 2500 employees. Numbers are pretty black and white; either they balance or they don't. People are a different animal. It's gray matter, all over the place. We're complex, and our issues aren't easily fixed with a balance sheet journal entry.

I choose working with the people, and I have never regretted it.

Back then, there were no degrees in human resources. Heck, they were still calling it personnel! So I joined ASPA—American Society for Personnel Administrators. That name says it all about the field at that time. We were a bunch of paper pushers. Later the name changed to SHRM—Society for Human Resource Management—as the world at work realized the importance of human capital and managing those critters! Through SHRM's relationship with HRCI (Human Resource Certification Institute), I became Professional in Human Resources-certified (PHR) in 1987, and in 1993, Senior Professional in Human Resources-certified (SPHR).

The 1993 certification was strategic: That was the last year you could be certified for life with only three recertifications needed in the future. My aversion to details includes keeping track of those credits needed to recertify! Luckily, I passed the tough exam, which had a 50% pass rate at the time. Later, I was invited to help write the questions for the SPHR exam, which I did for three years, and that was even harder than taking the test, if you can believe that! Here I was, cooped up for three days writing exam questions with a bunch of PhDs, wondering why little ole me was invited. Being the rebel I am, I wrote bleeding-edge questions, which quickly got shot down because the ideas were so new they weren't yet in textbooks I could cite as my references. I was using ideas that were just coming out from thought leaders like Kevin Wheeler, Marshall Goldsmith, and others to write my questions!

Throughout my career in HR, I have had an unquenched desire to learn all I could about leadership. I wanted to know what made one company such a joy to work in, and another your worst nightmare. I've worked for both. Sometimes I think working for one of the best ruined me: I knew what a great culture and working experience could be. I knew what it felt like to be excited about your work on Monday morning, instead of dreading it. When I didn't have that positive energy, I sorely missed it. Sometimes I could change that situation, and sometimes I was powerless: The egos involved were simply too big for me, the "HR Momma" to even consider attempting.

This book is simply about what I think works in the management of people. It is meant as a simple handbook for entrepreneurs or new folks in HR—anyone who cares about creating something that benefits all. It is definitely not rocket science. People are people; it's the environment and technologies that change. We still have the same human hearts, and we still want the same things. The various techniques and movements throughout the past decades all seem to have the same core principles, which I hope to share in this book.

I've been assessed to death, so know I tend to be optimistic, but it works for me! I'm a happy camper, and I enjoy my own company, but I'm not naive. There are always people who are going to disappoint you despite your best efforts (and sometimes even theirs). Let them stay in their stories. The principles I'm going to talk about in this book will benefit MOST people, but not all. Some will certainly upset the status quo, but do give them some thought. There is tons of research to back up these "radical" ideas!

To keep myself focused, I'll arrange this book starting with a concept Jim Collins's originated: getting the right people on your bus. But I'm going to add a few things, like making sure they're *sitting in the right seats, going to the same destination,* and *singing "Kumbaya"*! This analogy will encapsulate the most essential components of modern human resource management.

Please disagree or share your own experience with human resource management by sending an email to Corliss@HRMomma.com. I love expanding my own experience and learning new perspectives! Bring it on! HR Momma's experience is a drop in the bucket when it comes to the depth of our field. I'll be the first to say I'm no expert. My basis is just my own experience, my lust for reading organization development books, and my love of listening to HR folks with interesting ideas. Challenge me!

CHAPTER ONE

Getting the Right People on the Bus

> *"Nothing matters more in winning than getting the right people on the field. All the clever strategies and advanced technologies in the world are nowhere near as effective without great people to put them to work."*
>
> –Jack Welch, *Winning*

Perhaps the most important task of any business is hiring the right people. Why? If you don't do this right, it will affect all aspects of your business. Your culture will suffer if a team member isn't contributing as expected. And as you know, your bottom line will suffer. Costs of a mis-hire—including the huge recruiting expense, lost training time, and opportunity costs—add up. The adage "slow to hire, quick to fire" is good advice.

I just heard on the radio this week of a high tech company manager who was having problems filling positions. I thought,

"How interesting: We've got high unemployment, and the caller is talking about 230 jobs she's having a problem filling." It sounded like a paradox to me. She went on to explain that she had found applicants who had the technical skills, but they lacked the necessary soft skills, such as communicating well, teamwork, and collaboration.

It may not look like we have a talent shortage, but believe me, we do, and there is a huge lack of qualified *candidates*, not a shortage of applicants.

And what's most often missing is the ability to relate effectively with other people. I'm seeing more and more that relating is an essential skill that people are increasingly needing to be successful in their careers: Business is all about relationships, and relationships require relating! (Seriously, texting is too limited to be a successful "relating" tool.)

Soft skills like relating are becoming more and more important, especially for project managers. They're dealing with global pains and virtual pains. Did you know that seven percent of your communication is from the words used, 38 percent is the tone of voice, and 55 percent is body language? You miss a lot if you just rely on words. This is why e-mail communications so often cause problems. (Thank goodness we can use emoticons to express our moods! Kidding.)

So there are a lot of really smart people out there who can't relate to people and can't read people. They do things like going on and on giving a dry, dull presentation, putting people to sleep…but they don't notice the effect they're having. They simply don't have the social awareness part of emotional intelligence or the presentation skills to get their message across. This inability to relate is a real derailer for many people's careers.

So how do you actually find the right people who have all the right skills—hard and soft—to invite onto your company's bus?

How can you be sure you're getting qualified candidates, not just 200 applicants? Well, there are a lot of factors that go into making a good hire. Let's talk about some now—some you've heard about before, and others may be new to you.

Of course, everyone intends to hire the best person for any given job. We don't hire the wrong person on purpose. So what's going on here? From my experience in working with companies from start-ups to the Fortune 500, I see the same problems over and over, regardless of the company size or budget, or the intelligence of its leaders. Let me explain what is needed in order to succeed in the critical area of hiring.

A Strong Employment Brand

Many companies give tremendous thought and resources to their product or service brand and market penetration. Most give very little thought to their EMPLOYMENT brand. Yet if you can capture this brand successfully, you can use it to become an employer of choice, and you will have top talent eager to work at your company.

What is an employment brand? It's the experience a person—candidate or employee—has with your company. I'm talking about the *entire* experience, from how they are treated by the receptionist when they interview to their career path within the company once hired. Let me give you a few examples of good vs. awful experiences that make a difference in how your business is perceived.

Application: The Unfortunate Reality

You would be so surprised to know how many applicants are totally ignored. We may joke about the HR "black hole" for resumes, but this is not playing nice. It isn't professional, and it sends a terrible message that "we don't give a damn about people here." It takes a minute with email and applicant tracking systems (ATS) make it easy. I see it all the time—someone who was interviewed never hears back from the company! Sometimes the position has been "frozen," but no one communicated this. Calls aren't returned. Or worse, a message from the ATS conveys that the position is closed.

This is the first time a person will have experienced your culture! People tend to tell others about *negative* customer service experiences they have an average of 17 times, but they only tell people about their *positive* experiences a few times. It's imperative this first impression be considered part of your brand. It takes little effort to treat people with respect, even if your workload is heavy and you're overwhelmed. It will pay off for the future.

Application: The Ideal

Applicants applying for positions should be involved in a communication loop that explains their status in the hiring process. Whether they are not qualified or under consideration, they should be told immediately. If they come in for an interview, they should know what to expect next. Make sure people know where they stand with their application! Don't be rude and ignore them.

> Applicants applying for positions should be involved in a communication loop that explains their status in the hiring process.

At one company where nurses are always needed (and in shortage), applicants are taken on a brief tour when they complete an application and are qualified, even if there is no vacancy at the time. Building relationships with passive candidates prior to the time you need to hire is just plain smart recruiting. It just takes a minute to stay in touch with good employee prospects, just like you would on the customer side of business. With your ATS, you can communicate to your talent pool on a regular basis on what's happening in your business. Imagine receiving an email about an award you received for quality or community service. This builds your positive brand for the future, and you'll have top talent lined up wanting to work for you.

And Another Thing…The Recruiting Process

Another part of your brand is the recruiting process, from your website and social media to the offer letter and a new hire's on-boarding experience. Is your website easy to navigate and use to apply for a job? Do you have employee quotes about what it's like to work there? Many companies such as Cisco caught on to this method by allowing applicants to communicate with employees! How radical is that? And how brave and trusting. But you will see the importance of relationships throughout this book. Start understanding it now; it's critical for your brand, since it is people who experience your brand.

Choosing the Right Person for the Bus: The Hiring Process

Putting new talent on board is a series of tasks that need thoughtful consideration. Number one, it's expensive to make a hiring mistake in more ways you may know. In addition to the actual expenses of recruitment—advertising expense, time to review applicants, time spent phone screening, optional video interviewing, numerous folks' time interviewing on site, checking references—just to mention a few, there are costs involved in getting the employee on board and trained in your company's methodology, the costs of lost opportunity (that vacant sales position lost how much revenue?) and time needed from other employees to get the new person productive and contributing! Research shows a benchmark of 1½ times the annual salary as the cost of hire, and other expenses such as relocation and headhunter fees can raise those costs considerably. So with this great investment, you've got to do due diligence for each hire.

Have a Consistent Process

Candidates are on their dating behavior when they interview. It's your job to make sure you "get" them by whatever legal means possible, by making or completing some objective comparisons. It's also wise to keep things consistent when interviewing and accessing candidates. That consistency will avoid lawsuits down the road. (Yes, even non-employees can sue you! Insane, but true.)

Sourcing

Candidates can be found in more venues than ever before. Although most companies go

---

Active Candidates: These are the unemployed and the under-employed—people currently out of work or unhappy enough at their current employer to be actively seeking new jobs. They likely have up-to-date resumes, knowledge about their competition and their value in the marketplace, and may be using the services of a headhunter or career counselor to aid them in their job search.

Passive Candidates: These are currently employed people who don't have a pressing dissatisfaction with their employer or position. They aren't actively seeking jobs, so they likely don't have up-to-date resumes or know their value in the marketplace. In fact, they probably won't leave their current positions unless a job change would bring significant potential for advancement, an increase in salary and/or benefits, or other compelling benefits.

the route of advertising their new position through job boards, their corporate websites, etc., smart companies often don't need to incur that expense nowadays. Why? The number one source for candidates who actually *get* jobs is networking. More than 80 percent of new hires come via networking, actually! So how can you get on this bandwagon, and why would you want to, anyway?

There has been a perception in the past that the "passive" candidate is the best one. I'm not so sure, though, now that we've been seeing massive layoffs: even top talent may be looking for new opportunities because they lost their jobs when their former employer went under! That said, the job boards are full of mostly active candidates who are unemployed or underemployed. So, whether "active" or "passive," where are these candidates, and how can you connect with them?

Smart Sourcing Strategy #1: Employee Referral Programs

Many companies get their highest quality hires through an employee referral program. After all, employees today are well networked and know your culture. Don't underestimate the power of referrals! Everyone wins; the employee helps bring on the right talent in someone they know, the employer usually gets a quality hire because the new hire works hard to live up to their reputation and reward their friend's trust, and the new employee is satisfied and productive as a cultural "fit." Results are delivered, and everyone is happy!

The best way to assure your referral program is a success is to be sure that your company is one that employees are proud to bring talent to! No one, unless he is seeking revenge, would bring a friend into hell!

> *The best way to assure your referral program is a success is to be sure that your company is one that employees are proud to bring talent to!*

Also, make sure all referrals are treated well, and that communication to the referrer is open, often, and honest. They will not keep referring if there is a black hole and they (or their referral) never hear back on the decision.

It also helps if there is some sort of incentive, and this doesn't always need to mean dollars. In the past, especially with the booming tech industry, bonuses paid to employees for referrals were extravagant! Shoot, an employee could make more as a company headhunter than they do performing their job! But it doesn't need to be that way. At the high-tech start-up I worked at in the 80s, the company's very effective employee referral program only involved public thanks/recognition and the opportunity to have the "Headhunter Award," which was a shrunken head on an plaque! The employee could keep it until the next referral hire, when it would be passed on to the next employee who referred a successful applicant.

Smart Sourcing Strategy #2: Social Networking

Another venue for sourcing is social networking. Forward-thinking companies increasingly are using YouTube, Facebook, LinkedIn, and Twitter as recruiting tools. It makes sense, doesn't it? Networks like these are filled with professionals who put their credentials right out there, also allowing access to other information about themselves via their blogs, articles, white papers, and so on.

The new capital is your network. Never before have people been so able to connect with old friends and colleagues and to stay in touch—more than half of the people going to social networking apps looking for work are using their mobile phones to access the content. You would never hire a headhunter who didn't have connections in your industry—so you need to tap into the connections of your company's human capital via social media. Ask employees who are the thinkers, movers, and shakers in your industry after they attend conferences. Proactively connect with these people. Start relationships, and keep them up!

I remember that while I worked at *Hire.com* in Austin, Texas, it took awhile to convince customers to think beyond today's hire and into the future by building relationships with passive candidates. Through Hire's application, customers were encouraged to direct people to their company's career portal even from the front page! Once captured in a very brief registration process, candidates could opt in to receive matching jobs or information about the company. This huge branding opportunity, especially communicating about company awards, community involvement, green initiatives, etc., kept the business at top of mind for great applicants. And as it often happens, the day came when a passive candidate was ready to move on, and they applied! Forward-thinking companies often don't even require a resume, as they know passive candidates may not have an up-to-date resume handy. They make it easy, and they make it fast to get engaged in a dialog with potential employees!

Smart Sourcing Strategy #3: Your Website

Is your company's career webpage learning from social networking sites? Are you using social networking sites to invite people to your site and to learn more about your brand? Is your website engaging and interactive? Cisco even got their employees involved by creating opportunities for telephone interaction between applicants and employees, so questions could be asked and answered. They really pioneered that personal touch: Transparency! Unfortunately,

> *Are you using social networking sites to invite people to your site and to learn more about your brand?*

so many corporate websites are a huge hurdle for applicants, filled with redundant information that is for their convenience only (or stocked with keywords in obvious Search Engine Optimization (SEO) efforts).

Just as LinkedIn and other social media can build your brand and provide information that adds value, so can your website! Think about whether your site even appeals to your target hires, especially if you have opportunities for Gen Ys. If they think your technology and hiring processes are obsolete, they will move on to explore other companies that make it clear they'll have the chance to grow and expand on their skills. Applicants *do* look at websites as an indicator of your company's culture.

Take Action

The best ideas remain ideas until you take action on them. Think back on what you read in this chapter, make yourself a list of 3–5 action items, then take action!

For example: Review your career website in light of what I've shared with you in this chapter. Go through the online process of applying for a job.

Now, you list your own:

- _____

- _____

- _____

- _____

- _____

CHAPTER TWO

Getting the Right Person in the Right Seat

"The ability to make good decisions regarding people is one of the last reliable sources of competitive advantage, since very few companies are good at it."

–Peter Drucker

Unfortunately, employee engagement is rare in today's workforce. People have been burdened with tremendous workloads during layoffs or "rightsizing" organizational changes. They are trying to keep their heads above water, and they are working hard. But that's not engagement: True engagement is when employees give *discretionary* effort. They don't just perform work, they look to add a little

> *True engagement is when employees give discretionary effort. They don't just perform work, they look to add a little more value…*

more value by helping a teammate; suggesting a better way to improve a process, product, or service; or volunteering for projects. Even tiny things like picking up a piece of trash in the parking lot show that they care and are invested. It is "their" company.

Use Their Strengths to Keep Employees Engaged

I have met so many talented people who are sitting in the wrong seat. And the wrong seat just saps their energy and reduces their productivity, because it isn't a good match to their strengths. When Marcus Buckingham was at Gallup, he and his colleagues assessed millions of people with the Clifton StrengthsFinder™ assessment to determine their top five "strength themes." These themes describe what a person was born to do, be, and have—what they have natural talents for and even may have mastered in their lifetime. I like the StrengthsFinder tool myself, but whether you use Gallup's assessment or others, taking into account a person's strengths as much as possible ensures employee engagement and innovation. Take the time to match a person's strengths to the position. Adjust the position if you have to! Don't let job descriptions be static and confining.

Create a Job Profile

Before you can start the hiring process in earnest, it is essential to figure out exactly what you are looking for in the position. We're talking more than standard job descriptions now. So many job descriptions are about skills and to-do lists, and often they are not current anyway. Answer the questions, "Why was this job created in the first place?" and "Has it changed since then?"

Take the time to let the job talk by creating a roadmap and job benchmark that can be compared to final candidate's Talent

Assessment, which will show gaps between the two. In addition, interview questions are generated and if hired, the candidate gets a development plan to bridge those gaps. This keeps things objective, measurable and legally defensible. I like TriMetrix® HD, an assessment process that creates key accountabilities and a roadmap for how a person would be successful doing a particular job. This assessment identifies characteristics in several areas required for job success: behaviors, motivators/values, acumen (how one responds internally and externally to experiences), strengths, and competencies of the job. Whether you use a tool like TriMetrix or not, be very clear and specific about who would be a good fit for the position. That is the first step toward getting the right person sitting in that seat!

You should have at least three assessments for each person you are considering hiring: one that measures behaviors, another that describes what a person values, and another that shows what their strongest (and weakest) competencies are. Ideally, you would be able to compare top candidates' attributes to a benchmark of the attributes required for success in the job they're applying for.

> You should have at least three assessments for each person you are considering hiring: one that measures behaviors, another that describes what a person values, and another that shows what their strongest (and weakest) competencies are.

If you take the time to hire right now, it will save you many hours down the road. How much time does a manager spend working with non-performers? Some say 80 percent of their time is spent trying to help under-performers improve, leaving them with only 20 percent to develop their high potentials. Having a right fit new hire from the start will allow your team to go to new levels of excellence and performance, and business goals will be met in a timely manner.

The Interview Process

From the first initial contact with an applicant, which could be via that fantastic career portal you've invested in or during your phone call to further qualify them, the candidate is evaluating you, too! It's not just about you evaluating them! Keep this in mind while you interview: you are showing your employment brand everywhere.

> ...You are showing your employment brand everywhere.

Have the receptionist expect the person and call them by name when they arrive, ask if they need to use the restroom or have a beverage, and in general show some hospitality! The receptionist can also be your ally, giving you feedback on the candidate's behavior to strangers or people with "lesser authority." We all know receptionists and admins can be linchpins in any organization!

Before anyone is allowed to interview a candidate, make sure they are aware of current employment laws! HR needs to make sure any structured questions are legal, which means strictly job-related. Interviewers need to be aware of the red zones and techniques for steering clear even if the candidate goes into dangerous territory. For instance, provisions in the Americans with Disabilities Act (ADA) make disability-related topics totally off limits: Take it back to essential duties of a job, even if it seems cold to not inquire about that cast on their arm! (A candidate got hundreds of thousands of dollars when an interviewer asked him this… No lie!).

If the candidate will interview with multiple people, let the candidate know ahead of time whom they'll be meeting and each person's title. And please structure your interview questions so every person is not asking the same questions! How boring for the candidate. Why not have each interviewer assess a competency or two? For instance, HR could ask about culture, benefits, and compensation with the applicant; the hiring manager could cover how he/she manages the team, and the results that the job is expected to produce; and a peer could talk about the tools and resources available to do the job.

Have a group session, which applicant and all interviewers attend. This is a good way to cover key questions so they're not repeated over and over. You can ask the applicant to solve a job-related problem or give a presentation of some kind…any job-related task so you can see it performed. Some people know this as "The In-Box Exercise," in which applicants are given a task as if it's in their "in box" on the job and it needs action. For example, a person applying for a graphic design job might be briefed on a flier that needs to be made, then given a certain amount of time to come up with a draft idea or two. This type of interview can be very intimidating to the applicant, so be sure to inject some humor to keep things moving. I have also seen an applicant be put into a stressful situation intentionally so their under-stress behavior could be observed.

If you use a job benchmarking system, have your final candidates take assessments matched against that profile so you can see the gaps in real time and choose the candidate who most closely matches your job profile. One reason I like TriMetrix so much is that it gives you specific behavioral questions to ask based on the specific competencies, behaviors, and values required for success in the position. You will be able to make an objective, legally defensible selection.

Immediately after the interview, all interviewers need to check in while their observations are still fresh. Some companies have a sophisticated rating system people perceive as objective, yet we all are subjective in our thinking. Others just review their findings and vote. Either way works. Caution: Stay away from reasons for why they liked the fellow or lady so much! Focus on skills, knowledge, attitude, and value they will add to the team! Remember, even a terrible applicant can be on his or her best "dating" behavior OR your interviewers may be awful at interviewing!

> **Caution:** Stay away from reasons for why they liked the fellow or lady so much! Focus on skills, knowledge, attitude, and value they will add to the team!

If the team votes "yes," make a thorough reference check before you make any offer. It's easy to find people not on the applicant's reference list who have worked with the person. Know one thing: HR usually provides minimal information on former employees. With many employment activities, there is a "Catch 22." If a reference says something derogatory about the candidate, they could get sued for defamation. Yet employers also can get sued for "wrongful or negligent hiring" if they don't check people out fully before hiring! So that being said, a background check is a no-brainer. Checking references provided by the candidate is a no-brainer.

So is checking informally with other people who may have managed, worked with, or reported to the applicant, which can give you other valuable perspectives. Your mission should be to see if the person is a good fit for the position, not get dirt on him or her. When you are speaking with a reference, you can mention aspects of the job you're hiring for to try to discover how the applicant performed similar tasks or roles at other companies. Always keep reference checks job focused!

Extending Offers

It's just good business to write out offers. Your offer letter should explain reporting relationships, compensations (and quotas if sales), benefit effective dates, position (I love putting the results expected of the position rather than just the title), contingency of background checks and drug screen if required, expected start date, and a date by which the candidate needs to respond to the offer. Back in the heyday of high tech hiring, when we had a "rock star" candidate interviewing, we would have the offer letter waiting on the last interview! If the hiring manager concurred with other interviewers, HR handled the last interview with the candidate to really drive home what a great opportunity it was to work there. Imagine the candidate's pleasant surprise to go home with an offer!

During the interview process, we may have found out a candidate loved cognac or heard his children's names (no, we didn't ask!). That data became a valuable piece of information when we sent cognac or a cookie arrangement to their home, along with a note mentioning the person and his or her family members by name. How could they say no?

> Often candidates will have "buyer's remorse," even though they made a rational and right decision...
>
> They are jumping into the unknown, leaving the familiar. Reaffirm their decision.

The Friday before an employee starts is also a great time to call to reinforce in the new hire's mind that "yes" was the right decision and to express how excited you are to have the person joining the team. Why? Often candidates will have "buyer's remorse," even though they made a rational and right decision. They most likely had a going-away party with the people they have worked with quite a while, many of whom are good friends. They are jumping into the unknown, leaving the familiar. Reaffirm their decision.

Arriving at the Bus

It's hard to over-emphasize just how important that first day, those first hours, on a job can be. Think about those first seconds of meeting a person: You form an impression of him or her, often one that lasts forever. Recall your first day getting on the school bus…unless your Mom or Dad took you to school…what a strong first impression! First impression moments are forever etched in our minds from childhood on, especially at significant times in our lives. Make the most of your employee's first day.

What little things make a difference when it's start day for your employee? I know from experience what doesn't work—things that turn people off from day one. One person had to wait in the lobby for two hours; finally, he was taken to a dirty desk that was still filled with the last occupant's things. How delightful! Another employee's new boss was busy, so she was taken to her cubicle and told to "read all the manuals"…for TWO DAYS STRAIGHT! No lunch with the team or boss, no introductions to others, just total aloneness. She was totally ignored. *You aren't important to us* was the message she got, loud and clear. Compare that to:

- The receptionist once again greets you and says, "welcome to the team. We're so glad you joined us."

- Immediately, your manager comes out and personally takes you into the department, where people come up and says, "Hi John! We've been waiting for this day. Welcome!"

- When you finally arrive at your cubicle or office, there is a Lucky Bamboo plant (a symbol of career success) waiting for you with a personalized plaque attached to it. You see that there are new office supplies and the area is clean, and then you notice—your name sign is up already! You have business cards on the desk!

- Your new boss sits down and explains the process for getting you up to speed quickly. You're given an outline of what is going to happen next: a tour of the facility (what is where); an overview of the organizational chart and whom to go to for what information; and dates and times of the orientation program HR has prepared with help from the management team (who will participate). You notice lunch with the CEO is on the agenda! In other words, you were expected, and they're glad you said "yes"!

- Because you completed the job benchmarking profile, your developmental plan is all set. Any skill gaps are in writing, and a plan is in place to help you close the gap(s).

The Plan: Moving Forward

"The purpose of an organization is to enable Ordinary people to do Extraordinary things."

–Peter Drucker

Part of the orientation for any new hire should include a tour of the facility, explaining exactly what the mission of the company is, showing how work gets done, introducing the key players are, describing business objectives in the short-term and long-term, clarifying the values that drive behavior in the company,

> ...consider formally or informally assigning your new hire a "buddy" or partner as a go-to person for additional questions that will arise in the coming weeks.

and clearly explaining the new hire's role throughout. Introduce the new employee to each member of the team personally, and encourage interaction. You may consider formally or informally assigning your new hire a "buddy" or partner as a go-to person for additional questions that will arise in the coming weeks. (Hint: Consider pairing a Gen Y with a Boomer, as Gen Yers often are often perceived as clueless about the work world and reality.)

So often, new members of a team have to figure out the culture—what is important, what never to do or say, what's OK, and what's expected in this environment. These things frequently are learned by trial and error—why not save a lot of time and get them out on the table now? Be as open and transparent as appropriate for this stage.

Remember, it's the little efforts that make a big difference in employee attitudes about work. One employee I know received a personal note from the CEO along with her first paycheck, encouraging her to give it her all and be a contributor to the company's success. Keep an eye out for ways *you* can add a personal touch to communication with your employees, building real engagement from day one on.

And Now… A Little Advice for Employees

When I'm in my coaching role, people always ask me for advice about their career paths. Here are some thoughts I usually share with them. Feel free to pass this along to anyone you're coaching or mentoring.

Self-direct your personal development and career path.

Do not depend on your employer to do it for you. I do some volunteer work with unemployed people, as I'm also certified as a career coach. I've noticed that many people haven't improved their skills in 20 years—they haven't kept up with the skills needed today. You've got to take personal responsibility for growth and advancement.

> ...many people haven't improved their skills in 20 years—they haven't kept up with the skills needed today. You've got to take personal responsibility for growth and advancement.

Get to know all aspects of yourself through assessments, observation, and feedback.

Welcome feedback—both positive and constructive—as a gift, and take it seriously. Thank people for taking the time to give you feedback. In all you do, try to be yourself: You were born an original, don't die being a copy!

Discover your purpose and your unique talents, and find a place where you can use them often.

Don't stress out over knowing your purpose! Just ponder "what you do," and it will come to you! What do you do with your free time? I like the question, "What would you do if you knew you couldn't fail?" Questions like these really get your thinking juices flowing!

Emma Jones is the founder of Enterprise Nation, a London company that supports small businesses. She has discovered that people who pay attention to what they do when nobody is watching them (or even paying them) often end up as entrepreneurs. "I'm seeing quite an increase in the number of people turning a hobby into a business," she says. "You start innocently by making cakes or taking photos in your spare time. Friends and family admire the results and recommend you to others. Before you know it, you are your own boss and making a living from doing what you do."

Just act! De-emphasize finding that elusive passion and re-emphasize doing.

Look within.

Know that life and growing are processes that never end. Yes, "school" never ends! Strive to be your best self—using your unique talents and fulfilling your purpose.

Manage your inner chatter. It's essential to be aware of what you are saying to yourself in your own mind so that you can choose your path, rather than react to circumstances. You've got to check in on your attitude often and make adjustments when it's not serving you.

> It's essential to be aware of what you are saying to yourself in your own mind so that you can choose your path, rather than react to circumstances.

Set personal goals. The foundation of coaching and everything I do is setting goals. I was just working with someone this morning on my marketing plan for next year, figuring out what I want to see happen in my business. I am not a very detail-oriented person, yet I will write my vision and strategic imperatives down: what needs to be done in what month and that sort of thing. I then put it away for the year.

But guess what? Knowing where you want to go specifically enrolls the universe in making it happen. When I review my prior years' goals, I realize that I achieve mos[t] though I rarely reviewed them throughout th[e year?] Just writing down specific goals is that p[ower?] remembers. I see this in coaching all the tim[e and it continues] to excite me. When clients get clear on what [they want,] watch opportunity and preparedness align, events transpire to make their goals happen! (And often, it happens very quickly!)

There's a story I love in the book *What They Don't Teach You in the Harvard Business School,* by Mark McCormack, who describes a study conducted on students in the 1979 Harvard MBA program. In that year, the students were asked, "Have you set clear, written goals for your future and made plans to accomplish them?" Only three percent of the graduates had written goals and plans; 13 percent had goals, but they were not in writing; and a whopping 84 percent had no specific goals at all!

Ten years later, the members of the class were interviewed again, and the findings, while somewhat predictable, were nonetheless astonishing:

The 13 percent of the class who had set goals were earning, on average, twice as much as the 84 percent who had no goals at all.

The 3 percent who had clear, written goals were earning, on average, *ten times as much as the other 97 percent put together.*

Know that adversity and challenge are your friends.

They allow you to step up and see how great you are. Have some grit! You have to be the captain of your own ship or the driver of your bus, and never, ever give up. There are always options, and there are always changes you can make. You are so much more powerful than you think!

Figure out what *not* to do.

I love Tom Peters and Jim Collins, the management gurus of our time. They each have in their toolbox something Peters calls don't" list and Collins refers to as "stop doing" lists. Instead making a proverbial "to-do" list to drive your actions and focus your work, why not look at what holds you back (usually your weaknesses)? As Peters puts it, "What you decide not to do is probably more important than what you decide to do." The key insight here is that we spend too much time on addition and not nearly enough on subtraction. Yet it's only by taking away what doesn't matter that we can allow what does matter to really shine.

So make your own list. As Daniel Pink says in his book *Flip*, "After all, God didn't offer Moses a few paragraphs of prose on Mount Sinai, He presented his commandments as a list. And, as it happens, eight out of ten of them tell us what NOT to do."

Take Action

The best ideas remain ideas until you take action on them. Think back on what you read in this chapter, make yourself a list of 3–5 action items, then take action!

For example: Make your own "to-don't list."

Now, you list your own:

- _____

- _____

- _____

- _____

CHAPTER THREE

Getting Everyone Going to the Same Destination

"Of all the things that can boost inner work life, the most important is making progress in meaningful work. The power of progress is fundamental to human nature, but few managers understand it or know how to leverage progress to boost motivation."

–"The Power of Small Wins,"
Harvard Business Review, May 2011

Sometimes we take it for granted that employees know their employer's strategic plan, but often this information is only in the minds of the company's executives and leaders. However, great leaders

> *Great leaders know that their employees need to understand the vision and know what part they play in achieving strategically important outcomes.*

know that their employees need to understand the vision and know what part they play in achieving strategically important outcomes. The best leaders also know that the strongest ideas often come from the people actually *doing* the work!

Are you tapping into this vital knowledge source? Let me put it another way: Are you telling or asking when you speak with your employees?

When there are clearly articulated objectives related to an overall strategic plan, new employees find it helpful to know their part: how their contributions and efforts will matter. And they can be held accountable to these clear objectives...although they probably won't need that formal accountability if they're really engaged.

When I work with smaller teams and companies, I like to ask questions of each member, and I summarize their anonymous responses for an Executive Summary I present to the group. These questions probe them for their ideas about where the customer fits in, financial goals, interdepartmental cooperation, quality, current company goals, etc. I'm always amazed at how different the answers are! These things need to be clear and covered at company meetings and other venues to encourage and measure progress.

Your performance management system can help you narrow down the broader priorities of the company, as well as more specific personal goals for employees. While many leaders are using discretionary

> *While many leaders are using discretionary bonuses, they need to be awarded objectively and based on accomplishing the position's objectives related to the strategic plan. Rewarding what was accomplished—and how it was accomplished—is important.*

bonuses, they need to be awarded objectively and based on accomplishing the position's objectives related to the strategic plan. Rewarding what was accomplished—and how it was accomplished—is important. Was the employee an effective team member? Did he or she meet goals in a timely manner so others in the supply chain could accomplish theirs, too?

There is new thinking in the area of incentives, and it runs counter to all that has gone before! Motivation is an inside job... and surprisingly, it may be good to doubt ourselves a little. Most of us believe in the power of positive self-talk, often in the form of affirmations. (I know many of you are remembering the hilarious "Daily Affirmations with Stuart Smalley" on *Saturday Night Live*: "I'm good enough, I'm smart enough, and doggone it, people like me!") While there is a powerful place for affirmations, especially if one lacks in self-esteem, new thought suggests we introduce some doubt in our goals.

Healthy Doubts

Yes, doubts—questions like, "Can we do this?" and "Can we fix it?"—may actually be good! Pardon me, Norman Vincent Peale, Anthony Robbins, and all the Power of Attraction folks, but Dr. Dolores Albarracin and her University of Illinois team explored the differences between what they called "declarative" self talk (I WILL fix it!) and "interrogative" self talk (CAN I fix it?). Simply by asking one group to ponder *whether* they could complete their task and the other to *tell themselves they would* complete the task, they showed that the self-questioning group actually solved more problems!

Albarracin, now at the Annenberg School for Communication, describes it this way: "Setting goals and trying to achieve them, assumes, by definition, that there is a discrepancy between where you are and want to be. When you doubt, you probably achieve the right mindset. In addition, asking questions forces you to define if you really want something and probably think about what you want, even in the presence of obstacles."

So, doubting can be a good thing! Asking yourself, "Will I?" and your employees, "Can we?" creates an opening for valuable conversations and new ideas. Remember: Questions open, while declarations close.

Compensation

At the time this book goes to press, many governments are mandating austerity, hovering on the line between leanness and meanness. In education, there have been attempts to "pay for performance" (student performance, that is). Sounds like a good idea, right? Why wouldn't a student be motivated to make better grades if he thought he could make money doing it? Well, evidence shows it just doesn't work! In 2011, Roland Fryer of Harvard University published data that showed that paying students for results didn't increase achievement, and test scores actually dropped. No change in behavior results when you offer to pay students for their output and results (it does, however, increase when you offer to pay for improved inputs like attendance, book reading, behavior, and the like).

So what does this mean for coaxing performance in the business world?

Some experiments conducted by notable economists George Akerlof and Janet Yellen studied employers that did something different. Instead of paying prevailing wage, these companies gave a little more to their employees. They found that this practice helped attract better talent (getting the right people on the bus is job ONE!), reduced turnover, and boosted productivity and morale. In the longer term, the companies that paid their employees better outperformed their competitors! And yet Southwest Airlines is known to pay a little less than the market, but offer great perks and a great culture in which to work.

Money matters, for sure. The ideal scenario is one in which people are paid enough that the issue of money is off the table—in that case, they can focus on the work and other associated rewards, rather than the cash. For more insight on this, read Daniel Pink's book *Drive*, in which he writes, "This era of pragmatism is also turning out to be an era of paradox. Perhaps the best solution for progress in our age of austerity is to be a little less austere."

> The ideal scenario is one in which people are paid enough that the issue of money is off the table—in that case, they can focus on the work and other associated rewards, rather than the cash.

Many companies nowadays have even gone so far as to *eliminate commission on sales, folks*! You would think without commission, there would be no motivation, and without motivation, no sales results, right? Isn't money what drives competitive salespeople?

In my own experience (and I'll bet a ton of other HR professionals out there agree), I have seen people on even a fairly complex commission plan learn to "game the system," delaying sales to a more advantageous time for their pocketbooks. It's not that they were unethical; they were rational human beings responding logically to the structure of the commission system. Research has shown that when salespeople are motivated by "meeting quotas" or "paying their bills" they're much less successful than if motivated by the customer's wants and needs. It's hard to focus on customer needs and wants, though, if you're worried about

> It's hard to focus on customer needs and wants, though, if you're worried about putting food on your family's table because you're not making enough money.

putting food on your family's table because you're not making enough money.

Challenging the sanctity of commissioned sales can actually bring benefits no one expected: less management time spent figuring out the numbers, more meaningful and interesting work for salespeople, and increased teamwork, which is a rare thing in competitive environments! Collaboration is usually discouraged when there is nothing in it for the person helping. Comp plans can actually divide people. (And think about what it means to the customer! If you're making a purchase, wouldn't you like to feel as if everyone is working to achieve your satisfaction, rather than you're simply a step toward a salesperson's quota?!) After all, *business is about relationships.*

Time Off

As an HR practitioner, I know that figuring out employees' accrued or deserved vacation and tracking it can be a nightmare. I have to admit I'm enjoying reading about companies who have thrown traditional time-off policies out the window—with huge success! I know you're thinking this is a recipe for an anarchic stew, but think again.

In the U.S., we've become basically a knowledge economy. Manufacturing and many rote jobs have been outsourced and/or mechanized. We're paid for our thinking and "value add" to our companies. Yet with the proliferation of mobile devices and the expectation of 24/7 availability, we often feel we are betraying customers, colleagues left behind, and even our own work ethic if we turn off during our downtimes. This practice has had many bad results.

We never really get to recharge or be there for our families totally if we're tethered to technology. Stress-related issues are at an all-time high, and people increasingly are turning to pharmaceuticals to cope with anxiety, depression, and downright exhaustion. We've become workaholics. As a Baby Boomer, I can relate.

But at the end of the day, what really matters? Questions asked of hospice patients about what they would have done differently in their lives always result in answers related to wishing they had spent more quality time with their loved ones. As you've heard, no one's tombstone will read, "I wish I had spent more time at the office."

So what's a person to do with this conflict?

Let's look at what a few well-known companies have done to address this problem, and see what results they achieved when they took a risk.

Netflix: Freedom and Responsibility Reign

Netflix's holiday policy is to have no policy at all! They tried it the old way but found it was really at odds with how employees did their jobs. Often, they were responding to emails over the weekend, solving problems at night at home. Employers don't log in how many work hours employees are putting in (except those billable-hour folks, who get promoted for long hours). So Netflix explains in their "Reference Guide on our Freedom & Responsibility Culture" (look it up on the Internet if you don't believe me!): "We should focus on what people get done, not how many hours or days worked. Just as we don't have a nine-to-five day policy, we don't need a vacation policy." As long as managers know where their employees are and their work is covered, this ultra-flexible, freedom-intensive approach hasn't hurt the company. It even provides us a broader lesson about today's workplace. Employees crave autonomy. In fact, autonomy isn't the opposite of accountability—it's the pathway to it, according to Daniel Pink.

I love what Netflix's VP for Corporate Communications said: "Rules and policies and regulations and stipulations are innovation killers. People do their best work when they're unencumbered. If you're spending a lot of time accounting for the time you're spending, that's time you're not innovating." I had to chuckle when I read that Netflix doesn't have a clothing policy either, and (so far) no one has shown up to work naked!

In today's workplace, the link between the time you spend and the results you produce is cloudier. It's not just a matter of putting in face time. Outcomes and results are what matter.

Starting premises about workplace arrangements can shape employee behavior: "If we assume bad faith from the participants whose main purpose is to defend against that nasty behavior," writes Clay Shirky in his book *Cognitive Surplus: Creativity and Generosity in a Connected Age.* "We often foster the very behavior we're trying to deter." People will push the limits of formal rules, play the system, and search for every available loophole when the defenders aren't watching. Contrast that with a rule structure that assumes good faith…and therefore will actually encourage positive behavior.

Best Buy: Results-Only Working Environment

Also check out Best Buy's ROWE philosophy: ROWE stands for Results-Only Working Environment. Talk about radical! The Best Buy HR folks convinced management to allow employees some autonomy in their jobs, letting them to be accountable for their results no matter what time they spent in the office, what meetings they chose to attend, etc. You get the picture. They were accountable solely for RESULTS.

Cali Ressler is the co-creator of ROWE and co-author of *Why Work Sucks and How to Fix It*, in which she describes the art of autonomy and accountability. According to Ressler, Best Buy employees focus on results, not face time, along with:

- Encouraging proactive collaboration among employees to serve customers
- Eliminating waste and redundant activities
- Promoting better communication and customer service
- Being more productive, efficient, and nimble
- Fostering productive turnover: keeping the best talent and weeding out poor performers
- Using common sense
- Utilizing the office as a tool as opposed to a default location to show up to every day

Compare the two:

Traditional Work Environment	Results-Only Work Environment
I get rewarded for effort and time.	I get recognized and rewarded based on my performance.
We need more staff to do this.	How can we be more effective?
Who's going to cover?	We've got the work covered!
I went to 14 meetings this week.	I accomplished X this week.
I get six sick days/year.	I manage my time all of the time.
I get promoted based annually or based on tenure.	I get promoted and rewarded based on my performance.

So what happened as a result of Best Buy's new philosophy?

- Voluntary turnover rates went down as much as 90% on ROWE teams. For one team, this meant savings of $2.2 million over the course of two years.

- There was an average of 41% increase in productivity on ROWE teams.

- Individual and team capacity expanded significantly.

Coaches, Mentors, and Development

According to PricewaterhouseCoopers' (PwC) 2012 Global CEO Survey, 47 percent of company leaders forecast growth over the next few years, however only 30 percent believe they will have the talent necessary to accommodate that growth. Similarly, a Deloitte study found that 56 percent of corporate leaders are predicting a shortage in executive-level leadership skills in the near future. A comprehensive leadership development program can help ensure you already have the talent you need in place when the time comes. There are so many effective ways to build leadership skills—your own and your promising employees'.

Feedback and Coaching

We all have blind spots: We know what we know, or we know what we don't know…or we don't know what we know or don't know! And the higher up you go in an organization, the lonelier it can get, especially if you're looking for honest feedback. For a lot of employees, the risk of giving you honest feedback is too high, so they tell themselves, "I'm not going to tell the boss the truth, because if I do, there are going to be bad consequences. I'm going to tell him (or her) what he (or she) wants to hear." Using a 360° feedback process is a good first step in getting insights, but go further! It is so necessary today to have a coach on your side with whom you can discuss anything safely.

> We all have blind spots: We know what we know, or we know what we don't know…or we don't know what we know or don't know!

A good coach can expand what I call your "TWIST"—The Way I See Things. It may be that there is an elephant in the room (what isn't being said), or your behavior is being perceived differently from what you intend. Blind spots can be brought to your total awareness, and knowing what you "didn't know" can transform your interactions with other people and the results you get on your own and as part of a team. As a coach, I have an extensive library of resources that help people develop specific areas. When I'm coaching someone, we discuss ways to capitalize on and expand their talents—the characteristics they already possess that are uniquely theirs. Coaching is so powerful, and it delivers a huge return on investment, if clients are committed to the process and accountable for themselves.

You may have heard about or read Marshall Goldsmith, author of *What Got You Here Won't Get You There* and other great books about management and leadership. I love that he talks about that required commitment at the beginning of the first coaching meeting he has with a client; if he can tell somebody's not ready for it, he won't move forward with coaching! Coaching is especially valuable at the management and executive levels, because the higher up you get, the fewer sounding boards you have: you might have your spouse to talk to and perhaps you have a peer or sidekick there at work, but just having somebody objective to bounce ideas around with is valuable. To have somebody to mirror you, be honest with you, and act as your champion is invaluable! I think anybody who's in leadership can benefit from executive coaching to get clear about their own life focus, priorities, and practical goals. You do this kind of planning with a financial planner, so why not plan your life?

Mentoring: It's Not What You Think It Is

> *"Imagine what a harmonious world it could be if every single person, both young and old, shared a little of what he is good at doing."*
>
> —Quincy Jones, record producer and musician

"There are many ways to define mentoring," says Jeanne Meister, a founding partner of Future Workplace and co-author of *The 2020 Workplace: How Innovative Companies Attract, Develop &*

Keep Tomorrow's Employees Today. If you are working with an old definition, you may be confused about how to get the advice you need. Below are four common myths about mentoring: Knowing the truth about them can help you figure out whom to turn to and how.

Myth #1: You Have to Find One Perfect Mentor

It's actually quite rare these days that people get through their career with only one mentor. In fact, many people have several advisors they turn to. "In all likelihood, you'd benefit from having more than one developer," says Kathy E. Kram of the Boston University School of Management, who prefers the term *developmental network,* rather than *mentor.* "It's that handful of people who you can go to for advice and who you trust to have your best interests in mind," she explains. This network can be as large or small as you want, and it may even include your spouse or partner.

We all know that sometimes it's helpful to get a variety of perspectives on an issue you are facing. Meister and her co-author Karie Willyerd agree with Kram. "It's not uncommon for people to have many, many mentors," says Willyerd, former CLO of Sun Microsystems and co-founder of Future Workplace.

Myth #2: Mentoring Is a Formal Long-Term Relationship

Because the world moves fast, and people change jobs and careers more often than they did 20 or 40 years ago, a long-term advising relationship may be unrealistic and unnecessary. "Mentoring can be a one-hour mentoring session. We don't have to escalate it to a six-month or year-long event," says Willyerd. Instead of focusing on the long term, think of mentoring as something you access when you need it. "It may not be big agenda items that you're grappling with. You don't need to wait until you have some big thing in your career," says Meister. In today's world, she says,

> Instead of focusing on the long term, think of mentoring as something you access when you need it.

mentoring is "more like Twitter and less like having a psychotherapy session."

Of course, the advice and guidance you receive may be richer and more relevant if it comes from someone who knows you well and understands your goals. You still need to build relationships so that when you require advice, you have the trusted connections in place. However, there may be times when you look to people who don't know you as well (or at all) to get one-off counsel from an outsider's perspective. And in these cases, Willyerd suggests you may want to avoid using the word "mentor" altogether. "You can simply say, 'I'd really like to get your advice on something.'"

Myth #3: Mentoring Is for Junior People

Many people assume that they only need a mentor when they are first starting out in their careers. "Now we understand that people at every stage benefit from this kind of assistance," says Kram. In The 2020 Workplace, Meister and Willyerd talk about "reverse mentoring" in which a more junior person advises a senior person on something like a new technology.

The reality is that "There are lots of points in a corporate career when you need a mentor," according to Meister. Though you don't need an excuse for a mentor, and you shouldn't wait for a huge crisis to seek one out, transitions are particularly good times to seek out mentors. Whether you are making a career change, taking on a new role, or contemplating leaving a job, advice from someone who has done it before can be helpful. "You may need a mentor when the environment around you is changing rapidly and you haven't had a chance to keep up with the changes," says

Meister. "Or as you try to navigate the complexities of your organization," adds Willyerd.

Myth #4: Mentoring Is Something More Experienced People Do out of the Goodness of Their Hearts

"It can be an honor to ask someone to be a mentor," says Willyerd, but the respect isn't the only reason people agree to help. Mentoring can and should be useful to both parties involved. Before seeking out a mentor, think about what you have to offer him or her. Can you provide a unique perspective on the organization or his or her role? Do you bring valuable outside information that might help him or her be successful on the job? Whatever it is, be sure that you are clear with your prospective advisor about what's in it for him or her. This does not have to be

---

Mentoring Principles to Remember

Do:

- Build a cadre of people you can turn to for advice when you need it.
- Nurture relationships with people whose perspectives you respect.
- Think of mentoring as both a long-term and short-term arrangement.

Don't:

- Assume that because you are successful or experienced in your field that you don't need a mentor.
- Rely on one person to help guide you in your career.
- Expect to receive mentoring without providing anything in return.

a direct barter; even the promise of future help, if and when it's needed, can be enough to convince mentors to share their valuable time and energy.

So, Do *You* Need Mentoring?

Now that you have a better understanding of what mentoring can be, do you think *you* need it? A good place to start is looking at yourself. Take assessments so you really know yourself. Learn what you're best at—you may be surprised by your strengths—and what you could use development in. Figure out how your strengths will help you (and your weaknesses may hurt you) as you seek to achieve the results you have to produce. Ask yourself if you have the resources to handle the challenges…and if the answer is "no," it may be time to seek out a mentor (or several). Remember that mentoring can take many shapes and forms—the key is to find the right kind of advice from the right person or people at the right time.

Performance Reviews

Millennials, especially, want feedback and advice about growing their skills. In fact, PwC's study showed that younger workers prefer career development opportunities to bonuses by a ratio of 3 to 1. And not just at the yearly review. In my career, I've seen time and time again that this annual function is dreaded by employees and managers alike. That makes me wonder if we have it all wrong. Maybe providing timely feedback on

> *The newest generation of workers is used to all sorts of feedback in a landscape lush with electronic feedback. Then they show up in the feedback desert landscape that is usually the office.*

the fly is better for everyone than waiting for a structured, infrequent review. The newest generation of workers is used to all sorts of feedback in a landscape lush with electronic feedback. Then they show up in the feedback desert landscape that is usually the office.

Consider the Olympics. Olympic athletes get better with constant feedback—from coaches, dieticians, biofeedback equipment, video replays, and so on—and that's not a bad thing. We all need feedback on how we're doing if we are to be our best. This ethic of self-evaluation is a hallmark of superior athletes and musicians, but you can apply this idea to your work performance each month by comparing your goals to your actual performance and learning goals.

Set high standards and monitor! Ask your peers for their input. You don't need a formal 360° feedback process to accomplish this...just do it! Many bosses today see the Gen Ys and Millennials routinely coming into their offices looking for coaching, mentoring, and feedback to improve. I believe that's simply a good idea!

Putting Conflict to Work

At some companies, conflict is purposely avoided organization-wide. Emotions are natural—we're human—and people don't always agree on things. Typically, people either go silent, withholding their opinion; or they give it fiercely, defending their point of view as if they are under attack. Few of us were ever taught how to have a "good conflict." Our culture often suggests silence: many parenting maxims we all heard when we were kids illustrate this. Children should be "seen and not heard," and we're told to "hold your tongue," being reminded that "if you can't say anything nice, don't say anything at all."

> ...as adults, we often hold back our thoughts, because we conflate speaking up with causing conflict. They're not necessarily related at all.

We internalize these messages, and as adults, we often hold back our thoughts, because we conflate *speaking up* with *causing conflict*. They're not necessarily related at all. And let me tell you, not speaking up at work is a huge lost opportunity! Because we all have different perspectives, it can be critical to speak up with valid information that could influence a critical decision. Often, early in our careers, we spoke up, but the results made us vow never to do that again! This is especially true when the person you'd like to speak up to is in a position of power! For instance, if you're a nurse speaking up to a doctor ("Hey, you're about to amputate the wrong leg!"), or a co-pilot speaking up to the pilot ("Wow, it looks like the windows are icing up!"). Yet consequences of *not* speaking up in cases like that can be severe.

Why do we do this? What goes on in our heads when we don't speak up directly and also respectfully when our voice needs to be heard? We justify our silence to ourselves, minimizing the importance of our ideas and experiences by telling ourselves that it really isn't important, or that we're overreacting, or that we must not know all the information while the other person surely knows what they are doing. We think that gets us off the hook. On the flip side, we *maximize* the implications of speaking up: "I'll get fired...then lose my house...then my wife will leave me, and I'll be homeless and lonely." Either way, our minds tell us it makes sense to shut up. The risks of speaking up are way too huge.

Learning to deal effectively and respectfully with conflict is a core skill at any company, whether you're dealing with human lives or widgets. We think if we just keep quiet after resolving the consequences of not speaking up in our heads, the issues will just go away. When we don't talk it out, we act it out in ways that don't strengthen relationships (e.g., sarcasm).

Unfortunately, conflict has a way of never really going away. It interferes with sleep. Then it affects our productivity at work—obsessing over something just 10 minutes a day adds up to 40 hours in a work year! Multiply this week salary by the number of members on a team and you'll get an idea of the cost. It is huge.

Encouraging Your People to Speak up

There has been a lot of buzz lately about trust. It may be because of Ponzi schemes robbing victims of retirement funds or executives and politicians being prosecuted for ethical matters, or child abuse coming to light when it turns out other people knew about it for years and kept quiet. In a company or team, trust is the foundation! People have to have solid, observed evidence that if they do "contradict" you with a different angle or new data that doesn't support your vision, you will not shoot them down publicly, or worse, retaliate in some sneaky way (such as less desirable work, lost career opportunities, or lesser working conditions and privileges).

If you want your employees to have the commitment needed to accomplish goals, you need to let them be heard! Have an open mind, and probe for more information so people can have their say. Interestingly, even if you don't opt to go their way, they will be more committed to your way when they feel they have been heard.

Learning to do conflict well is a skill and skills can be learned. Personally, I like the *Crucial Conversation* model, because it revolves around creating safety so a dialogue (rather than a monologue) can take place. It's easy to learn skills that can create and maintain everyone's feeling of safety during a difficult conversation. If there is time before a conversation—and sometimes there isn't much—you can start to analyze what's really going on.

- Has a personal emotional trigger been pushed?
- Is this a one-time event, or a pattern that may be affecting the relationship?
- What is my involvement in this? Have I told myself a story (assume) that may not be true about what's happening?
- What don't I know?
- Why would a reasonable, rational, and decent person do this? How does anyone know another's motivation or intention?
- What do I really want for this relationship? Do we have any mutual purpose here?

I once had a young client, 23 years old, who was ready to quit her job (which she loved) because another team leader was encroaching on her team, breaking boundaries. She was ready to give up a lot over an interpersonal conflict! I asked if she was willing to work on her conflict skills, and she said, "yes." After education and practice, she held an important conversation with the other team leader. Now they're best friends!

The point? Sometimes we dread a difficult conversation so much, we talk ourselves out of having it! You know what I mean: You have a conversation with yourself about it ("She's not going to listen,…I'm going to lose my job…Maybe I'm doing something wrong…" and so on). And you scare yourself so much you don't stop to put your own thoughts into perspective. Once you give it an awkward try, you'll discover that you don't die! And you'll get better at it the next time you need to speak up. It's a skill we build upon over our lifetimes, and it's a critical skill in all our relationships!

Again, it's critical that you ensure there's a culture of trust within your organization and among its people. Without trust, you'll never have accurate feedback, great ideas will be overlooked, and teamwork will suffer. Trust is a relationship that has many aspects, but competence and character are its main components.

- **Competence** is an important trust factor because people need to know you are capable of doing a job or task when you say you will. It also means proactively alerting others when obstacles prevent that task accomplishment from happening.

- **Character** involves "walking your talk" and being authentic as a person. For a leader, this means being vulnerable, too. When a leader can say, "I screwed up," or, "I don't know the answer but will find out," or even, "I'm sorry," it's a huge deposit in their employees' emotional bank accounts.

We all have "accounts" within every relationship. We make "deposits" when we trust being real with someone. We also make deposits when we praise someone's specific work or give credit to them rather

> We all have "accounts" within every relationship. We make "deposits" when we trust being real with someone. We also make deposits when we praise someone's specific work or give credit to them rather than ourselves.

than ourselves. Then, when we need to make a "withdrawal" from that bank account—for say, constructive feedback to help them grow or be accountable—it doesn't overdraw the account. They know your intentions are good and they have trust in you.

Knowing someone has your back releases so much positive energy, which can be put back into our work. There is so much wasted time trying to cover our asses or kiss them, politicking our accomplishments to boost our career and good standing, making excuses why we shouldn't be held accountable, and engaging in destructive office gossip that it's a wonder we get any work done!

I explained to a recent leadership class that 10 minutes a day equals one week in a work year. I intended to show that little commitments in time towards a goal can make a difference. Later, in a coaching session, one leader complained that she had several people on her team who wanted a break in the morning *and* in the afternoon! That would be two weeks of time "wasted." If she trusted her employees, she would have had a different attitude about this. Maybe she would have understood about brain fatigue and the need for adults to refresh their thinking throughout the day. Or maybe she would have understood that making a social connection during the day versus operating nose to the grindstone all day would make for happier employees and build meaningful relationships within the organization (this is especially true for people-oriented behavioral styles). She needed to let go of the "control and command" mindset and move toward letting her employees have real personal accountability.

> ...let go of the "control and command" mindset and move toward letting [your] employees have real personal accountability.

Innovation & Creative Thinking

Our only real competitive advantage is innovation. There are countless ways to encourage creativity and innovation in yourself and others. One technique is doing the reverse of whatever you're doing now. Make the "Fisch Flip," used by Karl Fisch, a 22-year veteran teacher at a Denver high school. Fisch flipped the traditional teaching sequence of lecture during class and sending kids home with homework at night. Instead, he uploads his lectures on YouTube for his students to watch at home each night, and he uses class time to work on problems. Often, students get frustrated at home when they get stuck on a homework problem—and how many parents can be helpful with algebra? Not me! Fisch says he didn't come up with the idea, and I can't help but wonder why more schools aren't adopting it. Flipping melts calcified thinking and leads to solutions.

Author Seth Godin "flips" the traditional way of publishing his ideas. Instead of publishing a hardback first, then releasing a paperback or e-book, he goes FIRST to paperback or ebook, THEN hardback. Instead of having an employee going away party, consider having a welcome bash their first day. Cafes like Starbucks and Panera have become makeshift workplaces for independents and free agents to access free Internet for a cup of coffee or a meal, "flipping" the purpose of a restaurant: come work or have a meeting... and doesn't this coffee smell great? What is one process, practice, method, or model in your business or work life that you could flip?

Research about Creativity

For CEOs, creativity is now the most important leadership quality for success in business, outweighing even integrity and global thinking, according to a new study by IBM. The study is the largest known sample of one-on-one CEO interviews, with over 1,500 corporate heads and public sector leaders across 60 nations and 33 industries polled on what drives them in managing their companies in today's world.

Steven Tomasco, a manager at IBM Global Business Services, expressed surprise at this key finding about creativity, saying that "[it is] very interesting that coming off the worst economic conditions they'd ever seen, [CEOs] didn't fall back on management discipline, existing best practices, rigor, or operations. In fact, they [did] just the opposite."

In fact, about 60 percent of CEOs polled cited creativity as the most important leadership quality, compared with 52 percent for integrity and 35 percent for global thinking. Creative leaders are perceived as more prepared to break with the status quo of industry, enterprise and revenue models, and they are 81 percent more likely to rate innovation as a "crucial capability."

Without continual breakthroughs, Facebook, Google, Apple, Procter & Gamble, and GE couldn't sustain success. We were born with creativity and imagination, yet as the years went by, especially around adolescence, we began to stifle our creative impulses because we became more aware of and concerned about what other people think. As adults, we often are rewarded for being cautious and analytical. This tendency becomes even more pronounced as we join organizations that favor critical thinking. As we become mature contributors to corporate culture, we are continually rewarded for our analytical abilities.

Time for Independent Thinking

Many companies, like 3M, allow employees work time to pursue their own projects. This is how we got the "Post-It Note" and many other innovations. Research shows that people are faster and more creative when they tackle problems on behalf of others rather than for themselves. It gives distance and a new perspective. (Why not swap your problems? Today, we have crowdsourcing and websites that post problems for the world to solve.) Many of science's highest achievements happen through unsanctioned, unfunded, or unofficial work. Yet most of our business work is "commissioned."

Australian company Atlassian has what they call "FedEx Days," when employees get an allotted time to work on whatever they want. At the end of 24 hours, they have to show their results to the rest of the company in a fun, freewheeling company meeting. They were so successful, they went from doing this once a quarter to allowing 20 percent of employee's time to free exploration! Google also has had "20 percent time" since it was formed: That's how we got Google News and Gmail. Twitter has a "hack week," when all the engineers cast aside their regular work to explore things that interest them.

In "Reclaim Your Creative Confidence" (Harvard Business Review, December 2012), Tom Kelley and David Kelley describe strategies for rediscovering our innate creative thinking abilities. The authors are the manager and founder, respectively, of IDEO, an international design and innovation consultancy. They identify four common fears that block our best ideas from coming to fruition:

- **The Messy Unknown**—Looking at spreadsheets filled with focus-group data won't inspire breakthrough ideas. In the real and virtual worlds, you'll hear unexpected, outside-the-box comments. Even feedback from seemingly irrational people—the customers whose comments you think you really don't want to hear—can provide important insights.

- **Being Judged**—Most of us care deeply about what others think of us. While we don't mind being judged in some situations, we rarely risk our business-world egos. We don't want our bosses or peers to see us fail. Because gossip spreads quickly in the workplace, we stick to safe solutions and suggestions. We hang back, letting others take the risks. Unfortunately, this approach prevents us from unleashing our most creative ideas.

- **Taking the First Step**—Creative efforts are hardest at the beginning: writing the first sentence, making the first phone call, announcing the intended project. The first step can be anxiety-provoking and physically draining. The Kelleys' advice? Stop focusing on the huge overall picture, and find a small piece you can tackle right away. Give yourself a crazy deadline. Instead of "by the end of the week," try for "before lunch." The first step will seem much less daunting if you make it a tiny one and force yourself to do it now.

- **Losing Control**—Collaboration means losing complete control of your product, team and results. This is an enormous sacrifice, especially for control-oriented executives. But in reality, we have less control than we think. The downside of shunning collaboration is staying stuck with the same routines, products, and business models. In a rapidly changing world, being a lone wolf really isn't a viable option. If your business doesn't change, it won't sustain success in the long term. Look for appropriate opportunities to cede control and leverage different perspectives.

> *It's essential to carve out time for your employees to do non-commissioned work. It breeds innovation!*

The bottom line of all of this? It's essential to carve

out time for your employees to do non-commissioned work. It breeds innovation!

"Grit"

There has been talk about *grit* being a key attribute for leaders, too. How ironic that a back-to-basics approach carries the day. It turns out that good old-fashioned grit has been determined statistically to be the number-one indicator of high performance.

Research defining *grit* as "perseverance and passion for long-term goals" found that as a trait, grit had better predictability for success than IQ. The experts break grit down into these building blocks:

- A clear goal
- Determination despite others' doubts
- Self-confidence about figuring it out
- Humility about knowing it doesn't come easy
- Persistence despite fear
- Patience for the small stuff that obscures the path
- A code of ethics they live by
- Flexibility in the face of roadblocks
- A capacity for human connection and collaboration
- A recognition that accepting help does not equate to weakness
- A focus and appreciation of each step in the journey

- An appreciation of other people's grit
- A loyalty that never sacrifices connections along the way
- An inner strength that brings them to their goal

Believe it or not, you can actually screen for, measure, and build grit. The Grit Test, developed by researchers at the University of Pennsylvania, is a simple questionnaire that helps you determine your Grit Score. It's worth four minutes to find out how much mojo you and your team have so you can get about building more of it.

Engagement

"Engagement" certainly is a big buzzword these days! Remember, true engagement is when employees give discretionary effort on the job—they don't just show up, do their required tasks, then go home. Gallup brought it to light with their survey items. One key question was "At work I have the opportunity to do what I do best every day." This ties in with using your strengths as often as possible.

Purpose & Community

"Only those who have learned the power of sincere and selfless contribution experience life's deepest joy: true fulfillment."

—Anthony Robbins, author and speaker

It's not just members of Gen Y who want their companies to allow employees to have purpose and contribution in their communities: It's actually a business model that's taking hold. Some people call it BO-GOA, which stands for "Buy One, Give One Away." Companies are steering this concept in a new, potentially powerful direction. For example, TOMS® shoes donates a pair of shoes to a child in need for every pair of TOMS that are purchased. This community-mindedness may become the future of business. Employees love it, and customers do, too!

Traditionally, the buyer has benefited from the buy one, get one free arrangement, but that is the old normal. This social mission is downright competitive! We see glasses being donated when new ones are purchased, and food donated to animal shelters with dog food purchases.

> We've seen in the past decade what happens when the profit motive comes unhitched from the purpose motive. Commercial entities should stand for something and contribute to the world.

Why are so many BO-GOA companies springing up now? One reason is social media, which has allowed "up-starts" like TOMS to spread their message cheaply and to enlist their customer-benefactors as marketers. It's a good thing. It creates purpose. We've seen in the past decade what happens when the profit motive comes unhitched from the purpose motive. Commercial entities should stand for something and contribute to the world.

Whether you work for a social-minded company or not, introducing the "why" of what you do to employees can have a huge impact. Stories play an important role in helping employees see *why* they do the work they do. A powerful "why" can double performance. We crave knowing how our efforts contribute to a larger purpose. Try asking the people in your organization, "What's the purpose of this organization?" Do they know "why"?

Their answers will tell you if they're all going to the same destination on your bus.

Take Action

The best ideas remain ideas until you take action on them. Think back on what you read in this chapter, make yourself a list of 3–5 action items, then take action!

For example: "Flip" one process, practice, method, or model in your business or work life.

Now, you list your own:

- _____

- _____

- _____

- _____

Singing Kumbaya
(Keeping Those Happy Campers on the Bus)

Some people don't think humor belongs in the workplace, but I can't see why. There is a lot to be said about having some fun at work. Research shows that employee well being is inextricably tied to higher performance, which is inextricably tied to the bottom line, says Thomas Wright, the Jon Wefald Leadership Chair in business administration at Kansas State University. After controlling for age, gender, ethnicity, job tenure, and educational attainment, Wright has found that an employee's psychological well-being is a significant indicator of job performance.

Maybe you didn't need an academic study to tell you that psychologically healthy people make better decisions and have better interpersonal behavior. I didn't: It's practically a given.

It's no surprise that the number one course in Harvard University's history is on Happiness. There is a huge Positivity movement now, and I say, "It's about time!" Way too many people are on anti-depressants or self-medicating with drugs and alcohol, and I wonder what has happened that so many people in the U.S. are unhappy and dissatisfied with life.

Fun!

Sure, happiness is an inside job. Yes, you can learn to be happy. So why would you want to have more fun and humor at work—that's external, right? There is actually research available showing the effect of happiness on important business metrics such as talent retention, customer satisfaction, brand loyalty, and productivity. It makes for a more productive workforce, simple as that. Fun is part of any great company culture, and this will become increasingly true as Gen Ys mature and become leaders.

I'll never forget the fun we experienced at *Hire.com* in Austin, Texas, at the turn of the millennium. Because we worked hard, we played hard for stress relief and camaraderie. We got to know each other in a different way when we were having fun, and we saw creativity flourish. For example, a cross-functional team put on "Hire. Prom." We had a real prom, in decade dress with a photographer, a band, and rotating mirror ball. We had "Hire. Pong," our yearly Ping Pong tournament, in addition to Halloween costume contests, and so on, which were a riot! In today's corporate world that requires doing more with less, employees need a break.

"Kumbaya" is so necessary on the bus. Employees need a chance to do and be something totally different and to enjoy the ride! Personally, I have fun every day; it is a core value in my life and business. When I do work with teams, I have all sorts of crazy little toys that we play with to understand work concepts.

For instance, in one training session, we were talking about conflict. I have a little pig with a foam ball in its mouth; when you squeeze him, the ball pops out. This is exactly what happens when you're angry, and your words "pop out" because you don't have emotional self-regulation. Using a silly toy helped make a very serious point: Your words can't be taken back, and they can hurt people and relationships in a flash, depleting your emotional "piggy bank."

I just feel that life can be taken too seriously! Fun elevates your mood, raises your happiness factor, and helps you cope with challenges. Happiness is missing from so many people's work today, but it's time to reclaim it. Having fun isn't wasting time—there are just too many benefits to it.

When you allow fun events at work, you build community. People get to see another side of their teammates. One of Gallup's engagement questions is: "Do you have a best friend at work?" Allowing *ad hoc* teams to come up with events that are fun and engaging gives people permission to express themselves, and in turn, this builds relationships.

Another side effect of fun is it's a great stress reliever. Laughing pumps feel-good hormones and makes us feel alive in a new way, taking ourselves (and others) less seriously. The younger generations get this: They demand work-life balance, while Boomers like my peers have put their noses to the grindstone and become workaholics, often becoming severely hurt and bitter when laid off or feeling irrelevant later in their careers.

There are plenty of examples of respected companies that have fun. Check out the Zappos story that CEO Tony Hsieh wrote, providing a roadmap for fun and principles for building today's workplace culture. Facebook and Zappos are places where fun is apparent. Often, there are outlets for "play" provided: things like ping-pong tables, video gaming stations, snack lounges, or Intranets. Contests ranging from Halloween costumes to cubicle decoration for major (or made-up) holidays also add fun and creative expression at work.

Community Involvement

Another big trend in the new world of motivation, according to Daniel Pink, author of *Drive, Motivation 2.0*, is contributing to the community in a meaningful way. Employees can work side by side with their peers on a project that changes the world. Employee groups can do important projects for organizations like Habitat for Humanity, Dress for Success (providing work-appropriate clothing for underprivileged women going on job interviews), or Win-Win Resolutions (anti-bullying training for kids), just to name a few.

Positivity

It's interesting to see the idea of positive thinking can be applied to business. Positivity has attracted a lot of attention from scientists in recent years because of its link to health, long life, and success. They've discovered that apparently, there's more to "being positive" than just feeling good. And they've learned that there is a specific positivity zone in which teams excel. When positivity is a core part of interactions, it produces bottom-line results.

An organizational consultant from Brazil––Marcial Losada––has applied scientific parameters to studying how high performance groups work together. Using video cameras and specially programmed computers, Losada's research assistants recorded every statement made during team meetings they observed. Losada tracked three dimensions related to whether meeting participants' comments were:

1. Positive or negative

2. Self-focused or other-focused

3. Based on inquiry (asking questions) or advocacy (defending a point of view)

Based on independent data, he also classified which of these teams could be classified as high performing because of high scores on:

1. Profitability

2. Customer satisfaction ratings

3. Evaluations by superiors, peers, and subordinates

Based on the results, about 25 percent of the groups Losada studied qualified as high performing. Those teams also scored high in positivity: in fact, their positivity ratios were 6 to 1 (positivity to negativity). Overall, Losada discovered that those teams who perform well have positivity ratios of *at least* 3 to 1. Low performing teams had ratios well below 1 to 1; while mixed performance groups scored around 2 to 1. (Losada then applied mathematical analysis to his observations and identified a zone in which people work together to achieve maximum results: the Losada Zone.)

The high performing teams also had higher connectivity with each other. They asked questions as much as they defended their own views, and they cast their attention outward as much as inward. I am not one who loves mathematical analyses, but I really admire scientific application of rigorous study to social interactions. It's really the only way we can be certain which factors are important and which are simply "nice." In this case, science shows us that positive interactions occurring with at least a 3 to 1 ratio over negative interactions contribute "positively" to bottom line results.

A Good Relationship with YOU: The Leader

Remember, people don't leave companies, they leave bosses. The relationship between an employee and his or her manager is *the* most important one on the job. The best leaders know this, and they find a comfortable balance between being the coach and playing on the team.

People often ask me if I have a "Top Ten List" for leadership in the new workplace. Everybody loves a top ten, don't they? So without further ado, here is my list:

1. Leaders don't do the control and command thing–they are coaches.

The old way is just not working anymore (if it ever did!). It's no secret that other people, not just the leader, have great ideas. The team IQ is higher than the IQ of they smartest guy or gal on the team, so there should be a lot of synergy on teams. Great leaders tap into that team wisdom, and they do it by *asking* questions and being curious, rather than *telling*.

2. The leader sees his or her team as human beings rather than resources.

When you get to know each person on your team, you have a new understanding of where they're coming from, what motivates them, and where (and how) they want to grow. One way I do this is ask team members to answer some very revealing questions in front of the team. Surprisingly, they usually are eager to share. There is a saying that people don't care how much you know until they know how much you care, and that is so true. When you know

> *People leave their jobs more often because they don't respect their manager than for any other reason.*

> **Truths about Leadership**
>
> Taken from Steve Boehlke's book *50 Lessons for Leading For Those With Little Time For Reading.*
>
> - "Leadership is reading between the lines while others only skim the pages."
> - "Leadership is more about questions than answers."
> - "Leadership is passing the ball when you want to take the shot."
> - *"Leadership is making time when there is no time."*
> - "Leadership is not a matter of position."
> - "Leadership is recognizing that conflict can be creative."
> - "Leadership is validated only by others."
> - "Leadership is knowing that even heroes are human."
> - "Leadership is believing in others as much as yourself."
> - "Leadership is passionate pursuit of purpose."

your boss has your back and best interests, you'll give discretionary effort. That's really what engagement is all about. It is people giving discretionary effort, not just showing up from 8–5, doing their jobs and then going home. People leave their jobs more often because they don't respect their manager than any other reason. Poor managers are a roadblock in their career path and the cause of their dissatisfaction at work. So they move on, at great expense to their employers.

3. Leaders don't make it all about themselves.

They don't expend energy maintaining their own image; instead, they give recognition to others. When their team is successful, they look outward at the team and say, "The team—you—did it all." Don't be a poor leader who simply looks in the mirror, pats yourself on the back, and says, "Great job!" Give credit where it's due. It doesn't take anything away from you.

4. Leaders allow themselves to be vulnerable, to be real with their team.

I just love it when a leader says, "I screwed up, and here's how," or "I don't know the answer, but I'll find out," to help the team learn and to show that no one else knows it all. How can anyone keep up with all the data today? We can't, and that's why we should rely on team wisdom. Being vulnerable is one of the biggest things you can do to build trust—to let other people know you're a human being, too.

One beloved leader I know actually asked one of his direct reports to mentor him in an area he was developing. That energized the direct report—it was actually recognition in disguise. It allowed the employee to serve the leader in a new way that respected what the employee could contribute. Some human resources people may not agree, but I say don't treat everyone the same. People are diverse beings: Treat everyone fairly, but not the same.

> Some human resources people may not agree, but I say don't treat everyone the same. People are diverse beings: Treat everyone fairly, but not the same.

Great leaders are kind and empathetic, knowing that imperfect human beings show up at work often with a lot on their mind. If their relationship is right, meaning they have made what I call regular deposits in the emotional bank account with that person, they have earned the right to have a frank accountability discussion about performance. They can also make accommodations for critical life incidents for an employee. This flexibility and targeted accommodation builds fierce loyalties and strong bonds with their employee. The little things you do make the biggest difference, and people stay on the job because of that one important thing you did two years ago!

5. They give developmental opportunities to their staff and don't try to do it all themselves.

The younger generations thrive on challenging projects that will help them grow in their careers. A lot of times leaders think, "If I want it done right, I need to do it myself," and they've never learned the art of delegation…and it is an *art*. There are different levels of delegation, from the earliest approach of asking a new employee, "Why don't you do the research on this, and make a recommendation to me," on up to saying to a long-trusted employee, "Do the research, decide what we should do, and get back to me." You have to figure out what each employee is capable of, and develop that trust in a person to whom you are delegating.

People love it when you trust them by giving them assignments that really stretch their capabilities. True leadership is passing the ball when you want to make the shot. You've just got to be aware of those opportunities to help your people grow and at the right stage.

6. They ask for feedback.

I do a lot of multi-rater assessments, and I do team surveys. One of the lowest rated answers typically is the item "asks for feedback." Everyone needs feedback, even at top organizational levels—*especially* at top levels. It's the "Breakfast of Champions." I particularly like Marshall Goldsmith's process called "Feed Forward," an approach that focuses on the behavior you'd like to see in the future rather than focusing on the past (which can't be changed). Because I model giving constructive feedback to my coaching clients, they learn how to deliver feedback in a way that ensures people are receptive to it, understanding it's for their own good.

We think we know ourselves, yet we all have blind spots. To be able to manage ourselves, we need to know how others perceive events and ourselves. *You* know what your intentions are, but sometimes your actions don't seem to reflect your intentions. Everyone interprets what they see and hear (from us and others), telling themselves a story based on many assumptions, and believe that story is 100 percent right. But usually there is "the rest of the story," facts that they didn't know.

7. Leaders have EQ.

You may have heard about emotional intelligence, a concept popularized by Daniel Goleman's 1995 book by the same name. Lack of EQ can be a huge roadblock, and that's especially true if you have an anger management problem.

> *You can improve your scores in emotional intelligence, whereas your IQ is fixed. Luckily, research shows that EQ is more important than IQ.*

People can't hear you when you're shouting. Intimidation, including aggressive body language, is not a good management tool. You can learn to regulate your emotions, which form in your limbic system—your "lizard brain"—by engaging the more logical cerebral cortex part of your brain before speaking. That process of awareness is called "mastering your stories." You are a lot more effective if you can learn to do this. That's the good thing about emotional intelligence: You can improve your scores in emotional intelligence, whereas your IQ is fixed. Luckily, research shows EQ is more important than IQ.

8. They don't over-react to current realities.

I listen to a lot of great leaders talking about different subjects in different environments, and I've noticed something: they project optimism about the future and they create a vision worth working toward. In contrast, poor leaders get caught up in crisis mode and become reactive in whatever the current chaos is. Great leaders are all about seeking solutions from everyone to help get past the current situation. It's not that they're in denial, but they convey real clear expectations, holding themselves and their team accountable. They're just optimistic and positive about where they're going to land; they know that they are going to get through it. That positive certainty is vitally important to followers, who need and want stability.

9. They are learners.

The strongest leaders take time to sharpen the saw—to acquire new skills and knowledge. What you learned in college is obsolete! It's imperative you take time to be current in technology and your industry, upgrade your management skills, and make real effort at self-awareness. If time is scarce for you—like it is for most leaders—listen to books, read thought-leader's blogs, find ways to get current industry news tidbits, and ask questions. Find the time to stay current!

10. They recover well from mistakes.

The big difference between a winner and a loser is how the loser handles losing. Ask anyone with whom you have a close trusting relationship, such as your coach, mentor, or advisor: We've all had slips and slides, but the key factor in high achievement is the ability to bounce back from the low points. Resilience is an essential leadership trait. Especially in a "down" economy, we *can* be disappointed that things didn't work out the way we wanted them to, but we *can't* let

> The key factor in high achievement is the ability to bounce back from the low points. Resilience is an essential leadership trait.

that hold us back. There's a lesson in everything that happens to us. Performance under pressure includes the ability to stay calm, learn, adapt, and keep on going. That's really what separates the winners from the losers.

And a bonus: 10.5

Talk less, listen more.

Take Action

The best ideas remain ideas until you take action on them. Think back on what you read in this chapter, make yourself a list of 3–5 action items, then take action!

For example:

Make an effort at growing my self-awareness. Be able to objectively fill in these blanks:

- My biggest strength as a leader is _____.
- My greatest weakness as a leader is _____.

Now, you list a few other action items:

- _____

- _____

- _____

- _____

In Conclusion

Well, I hope you've learned a lot about what it takes to fill up your Good Bus. Some of the ideas may seem radical, but listen: they are working for other people, teams, and organizations! It's time to open our minds about what work means. We need to be curious about the human beings showing up every day and think about how we can make that experience beneficial for both employee and employer.

This isn't rocket science. You may have noticed most of what I've described isn't new. However, it may be challenging the *status quo*—"the way it's always been done." With work taking up 1/3 of our lives for many of us, we need to be aware of the local, national, and global demographics so we understand the changing pool of job applicants who will be leading our companies in a few years. We need to examine social science research to take a look at management practices and get rid of those that aren't working anymore.

The bottom line: It's a challenge to embrace the global economy, keep up with technology, and stay connected with top talent.

The only way to stay relevant is to be curious. Keep reading and learning from others. Take a risk: Listen to your employees.

Work can be meaningful, and you can have a wonderful ride on the road to personal and business accomplishments. This is my wish for you: Create a Good Bus and enjoy the ride!

Appendix

Suggested Reading List

(not inclusive!)

- *For Your Improvement*, by Michael Lombardo and Robert Eishinger
- *The Five Dysfunctions of a Team*, by Patrick Lencioni
- *The Leadership Pipeline*, by Ram Charan, Stephen Drotter, and James Noel
- *StrengthsFinder 2.0*, by Tom Rath
- *The Community of the Future*, by Frances Hesselbein, Marshall Goldsmith, Richard Beckhard, and Richard Schbert
- *Emotional Intelligence 2.0*, by Travis Bradberry and Jean Greaves
- *Crucial Conversations*, by Kerry Patterson, Joseph Grenny, Ron McMillan, and Al Switzler
- *Crucial Confrontations*, by Kerry Patterson, Joseph Grenny, Ron McMillan, and Al Switzler
- *Influencer*, by Kerry Patterson, Joseph Grenny, David Maxfield, Ron McMillian, and Al Switzler
- *Good to Great*, by Jim Collins

- *Getting Things Done*, by David Allen
- *The EQ Interview*, by Adele B. Lynn
- *Emotional Intelligence Activities*, by Adele B. Lynn
- *Transparency*, by Warren Bennis, Daniel Goldman, and James O'Toole
- *Drive*, by Daniel Pink
- *Mojo*, by Marshall Goldsmith
- *What Got You Here Won't Get You There*, by Marshall Goldsmith
- *Thinking, Fast and Slow*, by Daniel Kahneman
- *What Every Body Is Saying*, by Joe Navarro
- *The Growth Curve*, by James Fischer